Also by Ronald L. Hirsch:

Raising a Happy Child: A Practical Guide

How to Find Inner Peace

The Self in No Self: Buddhist Heresies and Other Lessons of a Buddhist Life

Making Your Way in Life as a Buddhist: A Practical Guide

Scratching the Itch: Getting to the Root of our Suffering

We STILL Hold These Truths: Preserving the Heart of American Democracy for the 21st Century

thepracticalbuddhist.com - a Buddhist blog

PreservingAnerucanValues.blogspot.com - a cultural criticism blog

Discover Your
Power
Shazam!

**A Handbook For Kids 10-18 and Young Adults
Who Don't Feel Good About Themselves**

Ronald L. Hirsch

"Discover Your Power," by Ronald L. Hirsch. ISBN 978-1-63868-211-0 (electronic); 978-1-63868-212-7 (softcover).

Published 2025 by Virtualbookworm.com Publishing Inc., P.O. Box 9949, College Station, TX 77842, US. ©2025, Ronald L. Hirsch. All rights reserved. No part of this publication may be reproduced, stored in a retrieval system, or transmitted in any form or by any means, electronic, mechanical, recording or otherwise, without the prior written permission of Ronald L. Hirsch.

To all the children and adults who suffer
because of the way the world has treated them.
And to the teachers who have guided me,
encouraged me to persevere,
and enabled me ultimately
to find the truths from within myself
and so free myself from my own suffering.

TABLE OF CONTENTS

Preface 1

Lesson 1: Your Swamp 3

Lesson 2: Why Do I Feel Down or Anxious 5

Lesson 3: You Were Born Essentially Perfect 9

Lesson 4: Who Am I? 13

Lesson 5: Can You Imagine? 17

Lesson 6: Humans Suffer - Animals in Nature Don't. Why? 21

Lesson 7: How a Child's Mind Develops 25

Lesson 8: Sticks and Stones 29

Lesson 9: Where Has Your True Self Been? 33

Lesson 10: Not Me! 35

Lesson 11: Freeing Yourself from Trauma 37

Lesson 12: Meditation - Bringing It All Together 41

Lesson 13: When Someone/ Something Pushes Your Buttons 45

Lesson 14: Celebrate Returning Home 47

Glossary 51

Appendix I - The Swamp 55

Preface

Adults like to think that childhood is a time of carefree existence, of innocence. That is nostalgia; it wasn't even true when they were children, and that sure isn't the way things are now!

So many children and young adults don't feel good about themselves; they are stressed out, anxious, insecure. If that describes you, it's because you, like so many other children and myself as a child, have been harmed by the way you were treated or other aspects of your **life experience**[1]—whether by family, peers, or the larger culture—regardless of intention and how much you were loved. You are not alone. The wounds can be seen in insecurity, fear, anxiety, anger, depression, and the list goes on. All of this happened through no fault of yours.

These wounds impact not only how you feel about yourself, but how you feel about those around you. And so these wounds have a huge impact on your ability to have beneficial, healthy relationships with yourself and others, to learn, and to develop your minds.

This course is designed to help you see yourself not as a collection of negative (or positive) traits that others have labeled you with your whole life, but to return home to your natural state, which is your heart, your **true self**—the amazing traits you were born with. Then you will be free of your wounds. And you will discover your power.

---

[1] See the Glossary for the definition of all words in **Bold** type. You will be exposed to some unfamiliar terms or thoughts in this book, but they will all be carefully explained to you. Give yourself time to absorb them.

It's important that you know where I'm coming from in developing this course. I suffered during my childhood and for most of my adult life because of things that I experienced as a child. I am not writing this as an outsider but as one of you.

I may have had great coping skills and so led an outwardly successful life, both professionally and personally. But inside there was always turmoil and I led a second, parallel, life which was quite dark.

I wasn't exposed to the truths I present in this booklet until I was in my 50s, and it took years of meditating to absorb them into my subconscious. So for much of my life I truly suffered. But now, thankfully, I no longer suffer; I no longer feel bad about myself.

I have written books and I blog to enable others to benefit from my experience. I have developed this book as a course to help you free yourself from your past and find peace.

It will take strength, courage, and discipline. But I have faith that once you understand that the self you have felt burdened with for most of your life is not the real you, that you will find the necessary strength and courage. within yourself to connect with your true self, your heart, and in doing so change your life and discover your power

May you find peace and happiness.

Lesson 1: Your Swamp

Swamps are places with murky water filled with decaying matter. But light shining on the swamp causes healthy trees and plants to grow and fish to thrive.

The swamp is an appropriate image to use when thinking about our minds, as the mind is often filled with negative, dark thoughts we have about ourselves. But if light is shone on our personal swamp, positive feelings about ourselves will grow.

For an example of how a middle school class saw their own swamp and its potential, see Appendix 1.

To set a baseline for this process you are about to undertake, answer the following questions:

What negative thoughts do you have about yourself or what negative emotions do you have?

What light could you shine on your own personal swamp to make positive thoughts grow?

Ronald Hirsch

What positive thoughts could you have about yourself?

Lesson 2: Why Do I Feel Down or Anxious

Children often ask, "Why do I feel anxious, why do I get down?" Those are important questions.

Children usually identify these and other feelings as coming from depression and other psychological conditions. But that still leaves the question of why you are depressed or otherwise upset.

The short answer is that negative stuff happened to you, often early in your childhood—you were treated repeatedly in a negative way or experienced a disturbing incident or serious illness that caused **trauma.**

Let me give you some examples from my own life. I grew up in a very loving family, but despite that, there were things that my parents did, as well as peers, that messed me up for most of my life.

- I knew I was different from other boys, I wasn't athletic and tough. While I was generally well-treated by my peers, some boys roughed me up at times, and some older boys once did something terrible to me which had sexual overtones and was very traumatic. Of course I could tell no one.

- I knew my father felt I wasn't normal—he actually said so—and so he sent me to the doctor, who said I was perfectly normal, but that didn't convince him; later he sent me to a psychiatrist.

- My father routinely yelled at me at dinner because he felt I was a fussy eater and would send me up to my room. As a result I became neurotic about eating with my friends' parents, throwing up before, and didn't grow out of it till my 20s.

- Once a week, my mother would go out to play cards with friends, leaving me alone once I was 8 or 9 till midnight or 1 am (my father worked very late). I was scared being alone and developed a fear of abandonment.

- I heard my parents arguing about me at times.

This may not sound like much compared to what some of you have experienced. But as a child, I reacted to all of this at a very gut level.

The result was that I didn't like myself. I felt that I wasn't loved, and indeed was unlovable. I felt there was something wrong with me. I was fearful. And I desperately wanted to be liked and loved.

And so throughout my adult life, although things looked well from the outside because I had strong coping skills - I was successful professionally and had loving friends - I was constantly in inner turmoil and, as I've said, I led a parallel life that was quite dark.

The story I just related is an example of how any trauma, as well as your mind's reaction to repeated less-serious incidents, are absorbed by your mind—as happens to everyone—and those negative thoughts and feelings become your **self-image**, your **ego**. Your mind becomes **programmed** to respond to situations the way it does.

And so the negative experiences produce negative thoughts that produce negative feelings that produce produce negative actions, whether you are 10 years old or 60. Even conditions such as Bipolar Disorder are largely a result of childhood trauma and stress.

What all of this means is that you have these feelings and reactions, these "conditions," because of your life experiences, the way you were treated, *not* because of the person you are. *You were not born with these feelings or conditions.*

The process of how we come to feel the way we do will be explained in greater detail as we go through this course. But know that you are not an isolated victim; this pattern affects everyone. Everyone—that means your parents, siblings, fellow students, even famous athletes, movie stars and world leaders—feel and act the way they do because of the way *they* were treated when they were children; the trauma they often experienced.

The world we live in is unfortunately not a very nurturing or friendly place to grow up. Quite the contrary.

But there is hope. You can place a barrier, a boundary, between this harmful past and you, between any negative forces you face now or will in the future and you. And by doing so be able to achieve your full potential.

You do that by discovering your power, by discovering your true self, your heart. Every lesson in this book is a step in helping you find your power, feel that you are strong and good, and love yourself. I wish you a good journey of self-discovery.

NOTE: After you've read each of the following lessons, think about what you've read, rereading the lesson over the next several days, becoming more comfortable with the concepts.

Do you agree or disagree with the following sentence:

I was not born with these feelings I have about myself.

       Agree   Disagree.

JOURNAL: Make a list of things you've experienced or have been said to you, in the past or recently, that make you feel anxious or down.

Lesson 3: You Were Born Essentially Perfect

Since you weren't born with these negative feelings about yourself, with these reactions or "conditions," what were you like when you were born?

When you were born, your mind was blank. All the stuff—the thoughts and feelings—that has filled your ego-mind came later from experiences you had, whether things that were said to you or things that happened or what you learned from the culture. So your mind as it is today is very different from the mind you had when you were born,

But you *were* born with a fully functional heart. Not just the physical organ, the source of your life's blood, but the symbol of your spirit, your natural state, the real you.

The heart has always, across all ages and all cultures, been thought of as being the source of good, of light, of strength. That is the real you; that's the person you were when you were born.

This distinction between your heart and your ego-mind is even represented in popular culture, in cartoons showing an angel sitting on one shoulder whispering good thoughts in your ear, and the devil sitting on the other shoulder whispering negative or mischievous thoughts in the other ear. The angel represents your heart while the devil represents your ego-mind.

Not only is your heart the real you, but you were born **essentially perfect**. "What?" you say.

The proof of that comes, believe it or not, from science. We know from science that every form of life, including humans, develops from a single fertilized cell that contains all the information to make it what it becomes —whether plant or animal—and how all its different parts work in concert to sustain life. Think of it, everything about your body and brain and its functioning was contained, was programmed, in the single cell from which your life started. Life, and that means *you*, is a miracle.

So it makes sense that the life force of the universe is embedded in each single cell from which all things grow. And that all things—human, animal, and plant—are essentially perfect at birth. When you think of the miracle of the transformation of that single cell, this is beyond logical.

Regardless what you believe the driving force in the universe is, whether it's God-driven or the laws of the universe/evolution, how could the truth be other than all things are at birth essentially perfect?

Now, of course I know that some people are born with physical or mental genetic abnormalities or damage caused by external forces such as drugs or stress while in the mother's womb, which is tragic, but they are still born essentially perfect human beings. "Perfect" here refers to one's spirit, the quality of your heart, not to one's physical attributes or mental strength.

Let me add something about the quality of the heart—it is pure, unemotional, but it is not unaware; it knows the truth. It is aware of what has happened to you, it recognizes the bad things in the world, it knows how things are, *but* instead of reacting to this knowledge with emotion, it reacts calmly.

Sit with this truth—that your heart is the real you and that we are all born essentially perfect, just like a plant or animal. It will probably take some time to apply that truth to yourself because this is a very different way of looking at things than we were raised with.

Let me again give you an example from my own life. I had a hard time wrapping my head around this idea of a real you. Even calling it my heart. What was that? I was obsessed with the turmoil within me; I couldn't imagine myself as someone else. I believed this truth, but I couldn't process it.

Then one day when I was meditating, a photo of myself as a toddler. that my mother had recently sent me from my baby book, came to me. And as soon as I saw that image, I knew that that smiling toddler, happy for no particular reason, innocent and pure, was the avatar of the real me. That was my heart. That was the person as I was born. And I cried.

That image and realization continues to be a huge help in separating me from the world of my ego-mind's emotions, creating a boundary, and relating to the real me. I encourage everyone to find a photo of yourself as a smiling toddler; if you don't have one, try to remember yourself in a happy moment as a toddler.

At this point, after reading this lesson and thinking about it, do you agree or disagree with the following statement:

The real you is your heart and we are all born essentially perfect.
     Agree   Disagree   Not sure

JOURNAL: How do you react to my statement that we are all born essentially perfect?

Lesson 4: Who Am I?

In the first lesson, I said that you feel the way you do because of the way your mind has reacted to your life experiences, not because of the person you are. And in the last lesson I referred to "the real you." You're probably scratching your head, "I am who I am."

Hard as it may be to believe, the real you is not who you think you are. The person you think you are is what's called the **false self**; it's a product of your ego-mind's reaction to your life experiences, as explained in Lesson 1. It is called "false" because it's formed by the impact of external events—what's been said to you, what you've experienced—it does not come from within you. Your mind was blank when you were born.

But that's the only self you've known your whole life. Your ego is the body suit, or perhaps straight-jacket is the more appropriate term, you walk around with every day. It is very real to you.

Instead, your **true self is** the person as you were born, your natural state, symbolized by your heart, as explained in Lesson 3. That is who you are and always will be, the real you, whether you are conscious of it or not. And what are the qualities of your heart? It is light, love, strength, courage, and wisdom. And what is wisdom? Wisdom is knowing that all feelings and judgments, self-criticisms and doubt, are a function of the ego-mind, not your heart, not the real you.

SHAZAM!. Your heart is the source of your power.

At first, as you read about this distinction between your false self and true self, between your ego-mind and your heart, it may be confusing; you may not be able to relate to it. But hopefully what I've said will open up the door just a little bit for you to be open to the possibility that the real you is not the person who's weighed you down all these years. Instead, the real you, your heart, is a source of light and love that will free you and empower you.

Note that this is not just some "new age" concept. A mainstream book for educators, *Circle Forward,* that is used in many schools, has as its first assumption that, "everyone has a self that is good, wise, powerful, and always there, always present, We refer to this self as the 'true' self or 'core' self. No matter what someone has done in the past and no matter what has happened to him or her in the past, the true self remains as good, wise, and powerful as the day they were born."

To start the process of understanding this distinction, let me quote some wise words that were spoken once by a great teacher: "If it causes you suffering, it is not you, it is not yours, it is not your self, for your self would not cause you suffering."

Think about it. Almost all the things that cause you suffering, that cause you to feel anxious or down—your feelings and emotions—are a result of how your ego-mind reacted and still reacts to things that you experience. By this definition, your feelings and emotions, and thus your ego-mind, cannot be your true self.

The rest of this course is devoted to helping you find the real you, connect with your heart, and discover the POWER in your true self.

Complete these sentences:

Your false self is

_____

_____

Your true self is

_____

_____

I am not the person as I was born because:

_____

_____

JOURNAL: When you read about your false self and your true self, what is your reaction?

Lesson 5: Can You Imagine?

You've just been exposed to a number of thoughts or concepts—that your ego-mind is your false self, that your heart is your true self, and that you were born essentially perfect—that probably made you stop and scratch your head.

While you understand that you are the way you are because of the stuff you've experienced as you were growing up and the way your mind reacted to these things—to say that this you is your false self? Who are you then? Or to say that your heart is the real you, your true self—you don't know your heart, you don't know what it is. And being born essentially perfect—that may seem hard to believe.

You have been given information that presents an unknown world to you, and people usually aren't comfortable with the unknown. And that's ok. To help you get more comfortable with these ideas, try the following exercises:

1. Close your eyes and pull up a picture of you as a smiling toddler, or if you don't have one, try to imagine what that smiling toddler looked like. Sit with that image for a few minutes.

   Keeping your eyes closed, sit with each of the following images for a few minutes.

2. See your toddler as the personification of your heart, the real you as you were born, your natural state, essentially perfect. Physically hug yourself and your toddler.

3. Imagine your heart to be filled with light, love, strength, courage, and wisdom.

4. Imagine what it would feel like if the positive force in your heart protected you from negative thoughts about yourself. There is nothing wrong with you.

5. Imagine turning your will and your life over to the care of this protective force inside you, rather than your ego-mind.

6. Imagine seeing yourself and the world around you through the "eyes" of your heart, full of positive energy and joy, and the neutrality of your senses (divorced from your ego-mind, your senses see things neutrally, just as they are).

7. Continuing to see things through the eyes of your heart, imagine yourself free of worries and concerns (these all come from the ego-mind) and instead full of faith in yourself and strength.

Repeat this exercise regularly over the next few days, weeks and months to increase your comfort level with these ideas and increase their impact. By repeating these exercises, you will slowly absorb this new perspective about yourself and put aside the negative thoughts you have lived with all these years.

Discover Your Power

JOURNAL:

Lesson 6: Humans Suffer - Animals in Nature Don't. Why?

In the previous lessons, you read the truth that your heart—which is light and love, strength, courage, and wisdom—is your true self, and that we're all born essentially perfect human beings. But obviously, the vast majority of people living and walking this Earth do not seem essentially perfect or even anything approaching it, and they do not express much love. What happened?

As explained earlier, what happened is the way people—meaning the human mind—react to life experiences. But why do people react as they do? Some answers can be found in looking at humans v animals (mammals in particular) in nature.

If we look at animals in nature—that is, not under the control of man—there is virtually no such thing as a neurotic or troubled animal.

Why? Many people would say it's because animals can't think; they're not smart. But we know that many animals are really quite smart, they can think, and they do have feelings.

Let me quote from a blog post I once wrote titled, "The Wisdom of Chickens," about my free range birds. "They are such good natured animals, always in a good mood, nothing disturbs them. Regardless what the weather ... heavy rain, a snow storm, or howling wind ... they are out there doing their thing, although they are smart and take shelter more often when the weather is bad. Even when they have had a scary brush with nature in the form of a hawk or other predator, while they may be very cautious that day, by the next they are back to their usual routine."

If ever there was a being that felt, observed, and perceived, but experienced everything without the intervention of their mind or emotion, that accepted things as being the way they are, it was my free-range chickens, and indeed all wild animals. (My chickens were wild in that they were free range; I did not control them.) Animals in nature, as opposed to those controlled by humans, are perfect examples of wisdom.

But if an animal is put in the hands of man, it can indeed become neurotic, as many household pets and other animals are.

So the difference is not a function of an inferior brain or less mental capacity. What then explains this difference between humans and animals? As you will see, it is mainly a function of how young animals, especially mammals, are raised and nurtured compared to humans.

A baby's or new-born mammal's need for nurturing, for unconditional love, is almost without limit. For both, birth, being thrust out of the womb, has to be a scary experience.

When an animal is born, it is typically licked all over by its mother and is always next to the mother's warmth. The young animal is made to feel secure,

When a baby is born, on the other hand, it is slapped on the behind, washed by a stranger, rolled up in a blanket and given to its mother to be held and fed before being put in a basinet by itself, surrounded by other screaming infants. From a baby's perspective, not a good experience.

So from the moment of its birth, a baby finds that its needs are not met, and so the first seeds of insecurity are sown. This pattern—needs not being met—continues during the baby's formative first years.

For an animal's mother, her babies are her first concern; nothing competes with that. So. for the period that animals stay with their mothers to be protected and taught life skills until they are ready to be on their own, their mother is constantly at their side, their well-being is her sole concern, and the lessons she teaches are those of nature.

Human mothers, parents, have broader concerns and so children have a different experience. It's not that parents don't love their child and shower it with attention; it's that the needs of the baby go beyond what most parents are able to give. Whether it's how they were raised, whether it's the demands of work or home, whether it's having their own problems to worry about … it's just the way it is.

So while children are growing up, living at home, they also learn life skills, but they are often not healthy ones because they come from our culture or the neuroses of their parents. Also, because of parents' own concerns and problems, they aren't always there for their children or they interact with them in ways that unintentionally harm them

Thus, when an animal is weaned and goes off on its own, it has had nothing but secure reinforcement from its mother, it knows its place in the world and everything it needs to do in order to survive. It knows life is a struggle; nature can be cruel. But an animal knows that such is life, and just like the chickens in my post, they go on with their life undisturbed.

For humans, life's scenario is very different, as we will see..

Ronald Hirsch

Answer the following questions:

Animals in nature are not neurotic.
    True False

Animals are raised in a way that makes them feel secure.
    True False

Humans are raised in a way that makes them feel insecure.
    True False

JOURNAL:

Lesson 7: How a Child's Mind Develops

You read how an animal is raised and grows up, what about a baby?

As a baby becomes a young child, proceeds through adolescence, and attains adulthood, the seed of insecurity that formed at birth grows to become a huge tumor inside each of us. Why?

By the time the ego develops around age 2 or 3, the child has a vast body of experience, much of it negative, that becomes labeled by the mind and forms the ego. That process forms the way we feel about ourselves and others, which stays pretty set throughout our lifetime because those feelings and perceptions are typically reinforced by our ongoing life experiences, both within the family and the broader society—whether it's the actual experience or the way our mind views the experience.

So the tumor of insecurity grows because it is fed by much of what we experience in life … in the home, in school, at work, and in the media. We are either told or learn that we are lacking in some way. Often we experience trauma.

For example, if a child is told over and over that he is bad or stupid, the child comes to believe that is the truth. That becomes the way the child views himself, and overcoming that later as he or she is growing up is challenging. The ego-mind will not allow the person to seriously entertain the idea that he is, in reality, good or intelligent. It becomes what's called a self-fulfilling prophecy.

Even if we are praised, it is often today accompanied by performance demands; we know how easy it is to fall from grace, and so successful people actually often have even greater insecurities than the average person because they have more to lose.

Scientific research has confirmed the process by which the mind determines how we react to situations and feel about ourselves.

Deep in the center of our brain is the amygdala, which has a powerful effect on our entire physical and mental well being. Throughout our lifetime the amygdala stores the situations it considers dangerous or threatening—whether physical or psychological. At the dawn of man, it was saber tooth tigers and fire; now the list includes when we aren't treated properly and many other non-life-threatening situations.

When the amygdala senses danger at any level, it reacts in a big way. It sends out the message for a massive change in our bodily functioning. Our heart beats faster, our lungs suck in more air to prepare to fight or to run. We feel apprehension and fear.

At the same time, the amygdala tries to shut down our frontal cortex—the source of rational thinking— so that it does not interfere with this emergency response. The amygdala in essence hijacks the thinking brain—and so controls how you react to a situation—in the belief that it can best preserve our lives with its storehouse of automatic defensive maneuvers. This is why you can't "think straight" when you are angry or gripped by fear.

The good news is that, as you will learn in this course, there are things you can do to regain control, both immediate and long term.

Discover Your Power

Answer the following questions:
Most humans are controlled by the way their mind reacts to experiences.
    True False

Do you often feel insecure, anxious?
    Yes No

Did people say things to you as you were growing up that affect how you feel about yourself today?
    Yes No

JOURNAL:

Lesson 8: Sticks and Stones

Let's say someone says something nasty to you. And as a result you feel upset. Why?

Despite the fact that you were born essentially perfect, with a heart that is light, love, faith, trust, compassion, strength, courage, and wisdom, you, as all children, came to be filled with negative thoughts that come from the outer world, not from within you. And when someone says something nasty to you, it resonates with those negative thoughts and so you feel bad.

These thoughts seem real, and in one sense they are—these experiences did happen and these thoughts are part of your ego-mind. But these thoughts are not real in that they don't represent your true self, not only because they are not inherent in you—they are the result of experiences—but because they say more about the other person or persons, not you, the object of comment or attack.

What do I mean by that? EXAMPLE: Someone calls you ugly or any other negative word; that's an example of the other person, because *he* feels insecure, trying to feel superior to you by belittling you.

Regardless whether you feel the word is in fact descriptive of you, the negativity expressed has nothing to do with you, the reason for expressing it has nothing to do with you. Yet you absorb the negativity.

And so, the child's saying that "sticks and stones may break my bones but words will never hurt me" is definitely not true. Words do hurt, terribly.

Unless you are in touch with your heart and its power; unless you are in your natural state. That creates a protective boundary between you and what you may experience. For example, your appearance may be plain but you're cool with that; that's your body and you love it. "Ugly" is a negative word and you do not relate to it at all; and so it cannot penetrate your boundary.

A teacher once said to me that if someone or something pushes your buttons, that's an expression of the other person's or society's trauma; it has nothing to do with you. So do not become angry or upset.

Can you wrap your head around what I've been saying? All the stuff that you identify with, all your feelings and perceptions, your anxiety and fears, are all crap that has been imposed on you by family, peers, or society, because of their own insecurity. And for some unknown reason, your mind has absorbed these feelings and made them yours..

But your true self is still within you, undisturbed, waiting to be rediscovered. That is your potential source of power.

Answer the following questions:

What are some words to describe your heart?

_____

_____

Do negative thoughts come from inside yourself (the first time) or from the outside?
     Inside Outside

When someone says something hurtful to you, is it really about you or is it about him?
     You Him

JOURNAL:

Lesson 9: Where Has Your True Self Been?

If your heart is your natural state, your true self, you may well ask where it has been all these years? Why has it not protected you? You may say you've never experienced that self.

Think about it though. Have you never had internal discussions between what we often call our good self and our bad self? Or as I mentioned earlier, you've probably seen cartoons with an angel sitting on someone's shoulder whispering good things in his ear, and the devil sitting on his other shoulder urging him to do mischievous things.

Well, where do you think the good self or the angel and its thoughts come from? Those are the thoughts of your heart, your true self. But they usually lose out to the thoughts of your ego-mind because it is more aggressive and forceful.

Or you might ask, quite naturally, "Why did my true self allow my ego-mind to ride roughshod over me and create this person who suffers?" A good question.

The answer is that the qualities of your heart are like a seed. They need to be watered and nurtured.

But most of us have received little of such nurturing as a child or adult. Instead all the negativity we experienced nurtured our ego-mind and it became an aggressive force, bowling over whatever light we still feel inside ourselves.

What you must do is start watering those good seeds. How? By meditating on the qualities of your heart and your connection with it. By affirming these qualities in you. By not allowing negative thoughts to occupy you.

I know, easier said than done. The next lessons give you some techniques to use in disassociating yourself from negative thoughts and replacing them with positive ones.

Answer these questions:
Describe an internal discussion you've had between your "good" and your "bad" self.
_____
_____
_____

What are some ways you can water the seeds of your heart's qualities?
_____
_____

JOURNAL:

Lesson 10: Not Me!

Here's a practice for you to try - Not me! Aware of the negative thoughts or feelings that had become part of me over the years, I began a practice of reciting these negative feelings, and after each one saying, with a flip of my arm and snap of my fingers, "Not me!"

I learned this from someone who called this practice, "peeling the onion." You are removing the layers of feeling that have burdened you to get to the real you.

So for example, here are some things I said:

Feeling fear—not me!
Feeling weak—not me!
Feeling there's something wrong with me—not me!
Not liking myself—not me!
Feeling I'm not deserving of being loved—not me!

I have to be frank and tell you this is not something you can change overnight. These feelings have become deeply rooted in your ego-mind. And so it will take time and lots of repetition to create new paths in your brain to free yourself from these thoughts. But you can do it. At some point you will even become aware when these thoughts arise and say, "I know you, but you're not me."

In Lesson 12, you will learn to add affirmations to your practice, which affirm positive thoughts about yourself.

JOURNAL and as an exercise, come up with a list of feelings that you understand now are not you, and say these "not me's" out loud to yourself every day.

Lesson 11: Freeing Yourself from Trauma

We all have experienced disturbing things in our lives that have caused us great emotional pain and suffering; this pain is called "trauma." See the glossary for a definition.

The negative thoughts and energy in your mind are to a large extent the result of how your mind reacted to these incidents and formed trauma. Think of the negative thoughts you have and you can probably connect many of them to specific incidents. To free yourself from those negative thoughts and energy, besides saying, "Not me!" you will also need to free yourself from your trauma.

Well, how in the world do you do that? There are many techniques to accomplish this, but I am going to give you three simple ones that I have used and still use: shine light and love on your trauma, shake trauma from your body, and bury your trauma.

But before you can do these exercises, you need to identify key trauma points in your life and key negative energies; don't relive the trauma, just name them. Not *everything* that has caused you trauma, just the key things that have given rise to negative energy. This is important because I have found that you can't free yourself from trauma, fear, or anything else without naming the specific thing.

Once you have your short list, you are ready to move forward. These practices should all be done while you are in a meditative state.

1. Call up your heart and ask it to shine its light and love on your trauma. When I do this, I visualize myself as a child *after*

experiencing the trauma; *do not visualize or relive the incident itself.* Repeat for each trauma.

Give your **inner child** permission to cry. Why do you have to give it permission? Because I found in exploring my trauma that my inner child did not cry at the time; the child repressed it.

This practice will dissolve, dissipate, the negative energy that has flowed from the trauma. How does this work? We are typically ashamed of the incident, of our role in it or our reaction to it. We don't like ourselves for it even if we were not at fault. Giving your inner child permission to cry and your heart's shining the light and love of compassion on the trauma begin to remove that negative energy.

2. Because trauma is not released when it is experienced, it buries into our bodies. Animals release themselves from such stress by shaking themselves.

There are various shaking exercises that have been developed for humans, but the simplest form is to just pat your arms and your torso like you were shaking dust out of them while reciting the negative energy that you are freeing yourself from. In my practice, I would say, "I shake all trauma, feeling week, feeling needy, not liking myself, feeling I am undeserving of love, feeling I am nobody from my body."

3. Bury your trauma with compassion; this is putting your trauma to rest. I also buried my tortured spirit. The first time I did this, I actually performed a ritual burial, but afterwards I just recited, "I bury my trauma and Ronnie's tortured spirit with compassion," when I was in a meditative state.

I recommend this be part of your meditation practice every day until you feel free of the trauma. Why? Because your trauma runs so deep and is so firmly rooted inside you, that it's not a once and done thing. In general, daily meditation is recommended for the same reason—our ego-mind is so powerful and its roots run so deep that you need to constantly put yourself in a good space where your mind cannot hijack you.

Answer the following questions:

What are the key trauma moments in your life?
_____
_____
_____
_____

What are the key negative energies that you have?
_____
_____
_____
_____

JOURNAL:

Lesson 12: Meditation - Bringing It All Together

What do you do with all this information, this knowledge? It's only useful to you if you find a way to absorb it, to make it part of you—every day.

Meditation is the way to do that and change the way you feel about yourself and the world around you. To come home to your natural state, the real you.

If you've never received meditation instruction, the basic method is:

1. Sit with proper erect posture (whether on a chair or floor cushion) — be respectful of yourself;
2. Concentrate, typically on a point on the floor;
3. Be aware of your breath going in and out;
4. Observe your thoughts but don't engage them; NOTE: be aware that when you meditate, everything that's on your mind will most likely come up; just let those thoughts pass through; and
5. All the while be aware of your surroundings.

Just as important is what meditation is not—it is not withdrawing from life, an escape. You're just quieting your mind. For more information on how to meditate, check out the many print and online resources

One of the reasons why people meditate is to provide a calm space where we don't feel our emotions, or better put, react to them. Where we can relax, un-stress.

That's of great value, but the deeper purpose of meditation is to help you discover who you are—what I've been talking about—by providing a space where you are free of your ego-mind.

So, to answer the question of what you do with this new information, you meditate on this idea that your heart is your natural state, the real you, your true self, not your ego-mind. This is the source of your power.

You also meditate to connect to your heart and to free yourself from trauma, as in the exercises I've given you.

Another thing you can do is recite affirmations as part of your meditation. What are affirmations? They are affirming statements you make about yourself. Here are some examples:

I previously suggested reciting a list of "not me's!"; while negative in form they are still affirmations. You are affirming these things are not true about you.

It's also good to affirm the positive form of your "not me's." For example, "I like myself," or "My true self is essentially perfect; there is nothing wrong with me," would be the positive form of saying that "I don't like myself," or "There's something wrong with me," are "not me."

Another good thing is to affirm the qualities of your heart. Another affirmation is: "I am sustained by the love of my heart."

Here is an example of what such a meditation might look like:

"I go deep within myself, past my thoughts, my learned experience, and return home to my natural state, my true self, my heart.

I see my toddler as the personification of my heart.

I ask my heart to protect me and I turn my will and my life over to its care.

I see myself and the world around me through the eyes of my heart—full of positive energy and joy, the neutrality of my senses, free of worries and concern, full of faith in me and strength.

I am aware that all my negative thoughts are a product of my ego-mind, and so I say to them all, "not me!" (name your key negative thoughts)

I open up my heart and embrace all aspects of my being and experience: the past—all childhood trauma, the present—all disappointments and emotions, and my future so nothing offends.

My heart shines its light and love on my trauma and so the negative energy that has flowed from my trauma dissolves, dissipates.

I bury my trauma and my tortured spirit with compassion.

I know instead that I love myself. I like myself. I am good. There is nothing wrong with me.

I am sustained by the love of my heart.

I know that my heart is filled with light and love, strength, courage, and wisdom, and it is the source of my power.

I embrace my true self and invite it into my subconscious, supplanting my ego-mind."

Let's see what this combined meditation feels like. DO THE MEDITATION.

Because your emotions are so powerful and deeply rooted, and you are trying to free yourself from their control by connecting with your heart, you should devote time to your meditation every day, ideally around the same time (I do mine when I first get up in the morning, so that nothing interferes with this important daily task).

Doing such meditations is an essential part of the process of connecting with your heart. But give the process time; because your negative feelings and emotions are deeply ingrained, it usually takes quite some time to be free of them. Don't expect it to result in immediately changing how you feel, especially when you're not in meditation.

But there is something you can do to help access that feeling of calm throughout the day. How would you like that?

I'm going to give you a short exercise you can do to bring your mind back to that calm space during the day. You should do this—it only takes a minute—in the morning before you leave home; at the end of each class before leaving when the bell rings; and at night before you go to bed.

THE EXERCISE: Close your eyes and breathe in deeply and quickly for 4 counts, roughly 4 seconds. When you breathe in, breathe in through your abdomen, not your chest, till your abdomen is fully extended. Breathe out slowly for 8 counts of the same duration, 8 seconds. That is, each of the 12 counts is the same duration, roughly a second.

Repeat 5 times; it will take you just about a minute.

This will center you, calm you. After the breathing exercise, you might recite one key thing from your meditation that resonates most with you.

JOURNAL:

Lesson 13: When Someone/ Something Pushes Your Buttons

What should you do when something happens that pushes your buttons? Stop immediately if you can. Stop your emotions; stop your thoughts. Literally, STOP. Then DO the short breathing exercise I gave you in the previous lesson.

Stopping is easier when you're feeling fear or anxiety; no one likes that. But anger is another matter. If the button pressed is anger, you, like many people, may like getting angry; it feels good to defend yourself, feeling self-righteous, so you may not want to stop.

You need to understand, however, that anger never hurts the other person, it just hurts you by getting you all upset. You need instead to do something to protect yourself, and you do that by being in a calm space and ignoring the other person. By being with your true self, you create a boundary. You feel what has happened but you don't react to it. Do the breathing exercise.

THAT is how you find your power. It is in not letting another person or situation get your goat. Similarly with fear and anxiety, you find your power by not letting the world upset you and drain you. Again, you've created a boundary.

A side benefit is that by ignoring the other person, not reacting, you're robbing them of their feeling of power. They want you to get angry; they want to upset you. So staying calm and ignoring them will cause them frustration.

When you are confronted with such a situation, the challenge is to stop before your emotions run away with you. Once your emotions, like a horse, are let out of the gate, there is no stopping until you drop from exhaustion. And this is not an exhaustion high, it is a debilitating feeling, feeling like crap.

You may have groaned at the thought of doing this breathing exercise throughout the day. But by doing this exercise repeatedly during the day, it is more likely that you will be able to use it when you really need it. Your emotions are deeply rooted and you need to give yourself all the help you can; you're training yourself to not be controlled by them.

Practice the exercise.

JOURNAL:

Lesson 14: Celebrate Returning Home

You have started a process of self-discovery. Of returning home to your natural state. Of discovering your heart, your true self, the real you. Of discovering the source of your POWER.

At the beginning of this course we identified that the negative thoughts you have come from the way your mind reacted to things you've experienced, whether it's things someone said to you, did to you, an illness you had, or just messages from the surrounding culture. These were all external impressions; they did not come from within you.

And we identified that these thoughts caused you to have negative feelings which were translated into negative actions.

In contrast to your mind now, which is filled with these negative thoughts, we identified that your mind when you were born was blank. It was a blank slate.

What you did have when you were born was your heart, not just the physical organ but the spirit that it symbolizes, which is light, love, strength, courage, and wisdom. This was your natural state when you were born, this is still the real you, your true self.

Understanding the distinction between mind and heart is the underlying truth that forms the basis for this course on discovering your power.

The message of this course is that if you want to discover your power, if you want to feel better about yourself, you have a choice. You can choose to return home to your natural state and connect to your heart, connect to its qualities and guidance, embracing it. You can choose to say "not me" to the negative thoughts you carry around with you that are a product of your ego-mind. And you can choose to free yourself from your trauma.

But it's not that simple because the ego-mind is so powerful and how you feel about yourself is so deeply rooted, making these choices is challenging. Just believing that the real you is not who you've always identified with is difficult.

If, after thinking about everything you've learned here, you still cannot see yourself free of your past, free of the thoughts in your ego-mind, and cannot make these choices, there is no blame. There is no failure. There is no weakness. That's just where you are at this stage of your life. Know though that the lessons of this course will always be available to you when and if you are able to entertain the possibility that a different life is possible for you.

If, however, you are aware that you are suffering because of the negative thoughts about yourself that are in your ego-mind, and you are aware that those thoughts came from the outer world not from within you, you will hopefully realize and embrace the idea that there is hope. That you can protect yourself from your past, your trauma, and the negative thoughts in your mind. And the source of that protection is the power you can find in your heart, the real you.

If you have started on the road to discovering your power, know that this road is not a short one. Never underestimate the power of your ego-mind. What you will need to do is repeat the lessons in this book—especially the lessons on "Can You Imagine?" "Not Me!" and "Freeing Yourself From Trauma"—by making them part of your daily meditation. I have been doing these exercises for years.

I need to emphasize the word, "daily." Think of this process as reprogramming yourself, but unlike a computer it is not once and done. The process needs to be repeated over and over again until the new paths you are establishing, the new synapses in your brain, are well established and supplant those that have been established by your mind during the course of your life. And that will take time. Be patient.

And now, at the end of this course, is a moment to celebrate what you have begun to discover. To celebrate the light, joy, strength, courage, and wisdom that is within you, that is the real you. To celebrate the special person you are, with your unique gifts. To celebrate your returning home to your natural state. Think of it as taking a vacation from yourself, your false self, your ego-mind.

JOURNAL here what you have begun to discover about yourself and your special gifts or talents. These can be very small or big things. There is no activity that is too small or too menial to be a gift or talent. Your gifts may deal with your school work, hobbies, work around the house, relationships, spirituality - any physical or mental activity you engage in.

Glossary

Ego - This is the part of the mind that controls/defines how you think about yourself and how you react to various situations. The word "ego" is often used in a negative way, meaning selfish. But the word "ego" here is value neutral and much broader. Also, the word "strong" is often associated with ego, as in "he has a strong ego." But that is misleading; the ego is certainly very powerful, but its self-perception can either be weak or strong, and even if strong there is usually an undercurrent of weakness. For example, insecurity is typically an aspect of ego even for people who appear strong. How is the ego formed? See the definition of "programmed."

Essentially perfect - When we are born, our spirit is unburdened by any of the negative experiences of life. The child is born with a heart that is light, love, faith, trust, compassion, humility, gratefulness, joy, contentment, strength, courage, and wisdom. That is an essentially perfect state of the spirit, the soul. A child may be born with physical or mental abnormalities or problems, but his or her heart or spirit is essentially perfect.

False Self - This is the ego formed within the mind. It is termed "false" because it is not the essentially perfect self that you were born with, that resulted from your development from a single cell to a human being. Instead, the false self is a product of the mind's reactions to your life experiences. The false self may seem very real and is deeply rooted in you; indeed it has been assumed by you to be your self-identity. But it is not.

Inner Child - Your inner child is the child within you that experienced all your childhood trauma. Your inner child is thus the home of your emotions. When you or an adult get upset, it's the inner child who is upset and who acts out. And so the inner child is alive and well in us all.

Life experiences - All the things that have happened to you, that you have experienced, during your life from the moment you were born, or even before while you were in your mother's womb. These experiences can involve family members, peers, strangers, media (not just electronic/digital but movies, books, TV, etc.) - basically anything that sends you a message either about who or what you are, your relationship with others, or what is expected of you or what you should expect.

Programmed - We experience things in life and our mind reacts. If we experience the same thing or type of thing repeatedly and we respond in a consistent manner, or if we experience trauma, our brain develops what's called "synapses," connections. Once synapses are formed, they determine how you react to similar situations in the future; think of them as being a path well-traveled. Each person is programmed differently because each person has a unique combination of life experiences, although many aspects of our programming may be similar because of common life experiences.

Self-image - How we see ourselves is a product of the ego and so also a product of the mind. It is firmly rooted in our life experiences. It is part of the false self.

Trauma - Trauma is the mind's psychological, emotional response to a deeply distressing experience. There are 3 types of experiences that cause trauma: physical (e.g. abuse, illness, an accident, disasters), emotional (e.g. parental abuse, bullying), and sexual. So when the text talks about freeing oneself from trauma, it is referring to the mind's reaction to the incident, not the incident itself.

True Self - This is the being you were when you were born, your natural state, the real you, as opposed to the person you became because of your mind's reaction to your life experiences, which is your false self. The qualities of the true self are embodied in the heart, which is the source of all good, is pure, and is strong. Fully stated, the heart is light, love, faith, trust, compassion, humility, gratefulness, joy, contentment, strength, courage, and wisdom.

Appendix I - The Swamp

This definition of the swamp came out of a "Discover Your Power" course taught in a middle school in 2023.

<u>As metaphor</u>:
A swamp is a place of dark, murky water and rotting material, But out of the swamp trees, flowers, turtles, and fish spring to life. What makes this possible is the light that comes from the sun and the oxygen in the air.

<u>Our personal swamp</u>:
1. Our swamp is a place of: depression, anxiety, feeling unloved, loneliness, fear, feeling small, insecurity, feeling weak, feeling invisible, low self-esteem, anger, feeling rejected, annoyance, sadness, bad thoughts, negativity, stress, feeling unlucky, feeling ignored, feeling scared, doubt, feeling we have no control.
2. The light we can shine on our swamp: Kindness, love, goodness, positive self-talk, joy, happiness
3. What grows out of our swamp when exposed to light:
feeling loved, positive energy, security, peacefulness, feeling healthy, feeling happy, feeling safe, feeling big, good self-esteem, feeling in control, hopeful, feeling strong, beauty, good thoughts, feeling good, feeling noticed, feeling worthy, feeling lovable, joyful, feeling listened to, positive peer and family relationships

www.ingramcontent.com/pod-product-compliance
Lightning Source LLC
Chambersburg PA
CBHW060857050426
42453CB00008B/1001